759.03 HAR

THE POCKET LIBRARY OF GREAT ART

Plate 1. SELF-PORTRAIT *(detail of color plate 12)*

SANDRO

BOTTICELLI

(1444/5–1510)

text by

FREDERICK HARTT

Associate Professor of the History of Art

Washington University, Saint Louis, Missouri

published by HARRY N. ABRAMS, INC., *in association*

with POCKET BOOKS, INC., *New York*

On the cover

PORTRAIT OF A YOUTH
Painted about 1490-95. 16 x 12"

National Gallery of Art, Washington, D. C.
(Mellon Collection)

Plate 2. MAGNIFICAT. *About 1485. Uffizi Gallery, Florence*

$\mathcal{SB.}$

No other Florentine painter can rival Botticelli's peculiar grace, his bewitching melody of line and pattern, his supple distortion of reality in the interests of poetic expression. Botticelli is little concerned with the problems of concrete existence. He admits us rather to a private world of passive, vicarious gratification. In such a realm no determined action seems quite worthwhile as long as a dreamy yearning—a kind of incurable spring-fever—can alternately satiate and re-excite both soul and sense.

The systematic art-historians of the last fifty years have had trouble accounting for Botticelli, wholly out of place in a Florence supposedly obsessed with the conquest of form and space, anatomy, perspective, and light. They took refuge in the notion of a throw-back to the Middle Ages, and presented Botticelli as a Gothic anachronism in the midst of the Renaissance.

More recently a new interpretation of Botticelli's art has grown up in the tradition of the Warburg Institute, culminating in the research of Ernst Gombrich. Botticelli's pictures were largely painted for leisure-loving Florentines who had inherited wealth originally gathered by a more energetic and austere generation. Gombrich has shown that the mythological subjects were based on the doctrines of Neoplatonic philosophers who formed a welcome ingredient of this cultivated villa society. In the light of their tortuous and kaleidoscopic ideas the intricately patterned style of Botticelli is no longer so hard to explain. No style could more perfectly express the unreality of Florentine Neoplatonism, striving to revive a largely imaginary antiquity, longing for an earthly beauty which could only palely reflect the ideal loveliness of a higher sphere. So far from being an anachronism, Botticelli's art is the most elevated expression of the new generation.

It is no accident that the virile style of Masaccio and the early Donatello had no followers in the later fifteenth century, or that Botticelli's art was rediscovered in Victorian England by a leisure class which

Plate 3. FORTITUDE. *1470. Uffizi Gallery, Florence*

Plate 4. TWO ZEPHYRS (*detail of color plate 18*)

had inherited, not created, its fortunes. Swinburne and Pater sought refuge from industrial reality in dreams of an impossible Renaissance, just as Botticelli's patrons had tried to re-create an impossible antiquity.

* * *

The artist's real name was Alessandro di Mariano Filipepi. *Botticello* ("little barrel") was the nickname of his tubby older brother, which eventually stuck to Sandro as well, in the plural form of a family surname. The father was a leatherworker. In his tax declaration of 1458 he mentions his thirteen-year-old son as weak and sickly, and just learning to read. According to Vasari, the sixteenth-century artist and writer, Sandro was "always unquiet, and never satisfied with schoolwork, neither reading, writing, nor arithmetic, so that his father, fed up with so extravagant a brain, as a last resort apprenticed him to a goldsmith"—probably another brother, Antonio. Somewhat later the lad may have been sent to study painting with Fra Filippo Lippi.

Sandro's first dated work was painted when he was twenty-six, an age which had found such painters as Masaccio and Castagno at the height of their powers. Vasari tells us that Botticelli "loved beyond measure those that he knew were connoisseurs of art, and that he earned a great deal." Nonetheless, he continued living in his father's house in the Via della Porcellana, and according to the old man, painted "when he felt like it." No woman's name was ever connected with his. When asked why he never married, he said that he dreamed about marriage once, and woke so terrified that he walked the city all night.

Plate 5. SAINT SEBASTIAN. *1474*
Kaiser Friedrich Museum, Berlin

Among Botticelli's neighbors were the Vespucci family, one member of which procured him an *entrée* with the even wealthier Medici, and another of whom, Amerigo, gave the New World its name. For this family he painted the allegory *Mars and Venus* (plate 27). But the next door neighbor was less agreeable. He ran a cloth factory, making so much noise that the passive, sensitive personality of the artist found work very difficult.

After the Pazzi conspiracy of 1478, Botticelli was commissioned to paint in fresco portraits of the executed traitors, hanging by one leg from the battlements of the Bargello, the Florentine police headquarters. In 1481 Pope Sixtus IV called him to Rome to paint, with the greatest artists of the day, a series of frescoes around the walls of the new Sistine Chapel.

But the sands were running out for the humanists and their patrons. Lorenzo de' Medici, the Magnificent, uncrowned ruler of Florence, died in 1492. Already the great Dominican preacher, Savonarola, had seen fiery visions of the sword of God lifted over Florence. His voice terrified weeping crowds in the cathedral with prophecies of punishment and destruction. In 1494 the armies of the king of France entered the city, and Piero de' Medici, son of Lorenzo, fled. A mob sacked the Medici palace and destroyed Botticelli's frescoes on the walls of the Bargello. The artist's chief patron, Lorenzo di Pierfrancesco de' Medici, second cousin to the dead *Magnifico,* maintained his position through intrigue with the French king, but for Botticelli the strain must have been unendurable.

He joined the followers of Savonarola (the *Piag-*

Plate 6. PALLAS AND THE CENTAUR. *About 1488*
Uffizi Gallery, Florence

noni or "weepers"), and may have brought some of his own nudes to the bonfires of vanities organized by the fanatical monk. At one time the artist had to agree before a notary not to have any more violent tiffs with a neighbor about Savonarola. His brother Simone, who signed a petition to Alexander VI to lift the excommunication of the Dominican friar, relates that Botticelli's studio became a meeting place for *Piagnoni*. This is the period when Sandro conceived his great series of illustrations for Dante's *Divine Comedy* (see plates 43 & 44).

The execution of Savonarola in 1498 resulted in the banishment of Simone, but not of Botticelli whom his brother accused of backsliding. However this may be, the painter's previous style was swept out of existence along with the class for which he had worked. The emotional tensions aroused by Savonarola and by the crisis threatening Italy at the turn of the century resulted in a new and mystical phase. But Botticelli could not absorb the High Renaissance style now being forged by Leonardo, Michelangelo, and Raphael. After 1500 he painted little. Isabella d'Este considered inviting him to take part in the painting of her celebrated Grotta, and then rejected him. In 1504 he was a member of the commission to select a site for Michelangelo's *David*, but his recommendations were not accepted. Vasari relates that Botticelli was prematurely decrepit, and walked with two canes. He died in 1510 at sixty-six, and was buried in the Church of Ognissanti where thirty years before he had painted the ecstatic Saint Augustine.

Plate 7. THE DEATH OF HOLOFERNES. *1470-72*
Uffizi Gallery, Florence

Plate 8. SAINT AUGUSTINE. *Fresco, 1480*
Church of Ognissanti, Florence

COLOR PLATES

PLATE 9

Painted about 1470

PORTRAIT OF A MAN WITH A MEDAL

Uffizi Gallery, Florence

22¾ x 14¼″

Although he holds a medal portraying Cosimo de' Medici, this young man has never been identified. At first sight one is tempted to think that the sharp discrepancy in the level of the eyes is an irregularity of the sitter's face. Actually, this peculiarity turns up again and again in Botticelli's work. The dislocation is further emphasized by the convex silhouette of hat and hair at the left, contrasted with the sharp inward angle at the right, and by the curious twist of the hands around the medal.

The unforgettable face is suffused with a brooding melancholy which probably pertains more to Botticelli than to the sitter. The richly modeled features and hands have a strong sculptural quality which the artist was soon to relinquish. But the landscape is surprisingly flattened. The plain and the river are treated almost as in a map, and their contours are vividly played off against the undulating mass of hair.

PLATE 10

Painted about 1470

JUDITH

Uffizi Gallery, Florence

12½ x 9½"

This tiny panel was once paired with another, which represented the decapitated Holofernes in his tent (plate 7). An olive branch in her left hand and a sword in her right, Judith tiptoes down the hill while gazing back toward the scene of her terrible deed. The maidservant follows her, carrying the head in a basket. The cruelty and violence of the subject are strangely subdued. The figures move with an enchanted lightness, and the severed head seems still asleep. Instead of the pride of victory Judith's expression discloses only a gentle poignancy.

Although the influence of Filippo Lippi is evident here, the proportions are already Botticelli's own. Arms and waists are unnaturally long, and through both figures runs a swaying, curving motion. The drapery is designed more to enhance the rhythmic grace of the figures than to imitate the real behavior of cloth in a breeze. The dream-like unreality of the scene is increased by the mysterious contrast in scale between the two women and the microscopic armies at their feet.

PLATE II

Painted about 1470

THE MADONNA OF THE EUCHARIST

Isabella Stewart Gardner Museum, Boston

$33\frac{1}{8} \times 25\frac{5}{8}''$

The youthful artist has here taken up a common
Renaissance theme, the Madonna and Child so represented as to foreshadow the Passion and death of
Christ. A ministering angel holds forth ears of wheat
and bunches of grapes, symbolizing the body and
blood of Christ as preserved in the bread and wine
of the Mass. Both the religious doctrine and the tragic
prophecy are muted to an elegiac melancholy. Mary
plucks an ear of wheat from the symbolic bouquet.
The Child, enfolded in a cloth like that which will
wrap Him in the tomb, extends His hand to receive the
fruit of His sacrifice, while the angel looks gravely
down. The pale dignity of the faces is enhanced by
the soft light and shade gliding over them. The repeti-
tion of the curving drapery lines in the forms of the
distant landscape binds the composition together.

Painted about 1475

THE ADORATION OF THE MAGI

Uffizi Gallery, Florence

43¾ x 52¾"

The Holy Family, with the Star of Bethlehem hovering over them, have sought shelter in a shed supported half on ruins and half on rocks. The peacock at the right symbolizes the eternal life gained by the new believers. The figures are scattered loosely through this informal composition as if actually gathered before a family altar. Profiles and foreshortened views of faces are juxtaposed so as to create a ripple of activity throughout the crowd. Some figures are lost in contemplation of the mystery, some engaged in disputation about its meaning, some gazing outward toward the observer.

In this *Adoration,* one of five representations of the subject by Botticelli which have been preserved (see plate 22), there are at least two identifiable portraits. The first king in black and gold is probably Cosimo de' Medici, who died before this picture could have been painted. And the moody young man with heavy eyes and sensual lips at the extreme right seems to be Botticelli himself at about thirty (see plate 1).

Plates 13 & 14
details of
THE ADORATION
OF THE MAGI

PLATE 15

Painted about 1478

PORTRAIT OF GIULIANO DE' MEDICI

Kaiser Friedrich Museum, Berlin

$21\frac{1}{4} \times 14\frac{1}{8}''$

Most of Botticelli's male sitters look out toward the spectator as though moved to self-revelation. But his portraits of Giuliano de' Medici show the young man from one side, gazing downward, withdrawn and aloof. For Giuliano was murdered in the Pazzi conspiracy of 1478, and the portraits were done from the death mask.

In all the surviving versions, Botticelli has emphasized an expression of great hauteur and strong tension. The contours are unusually incisive. The profile, with its high forehead, aristocratic brows, long nose, and jutting chin, is as sharp as if carved in stone.

PLATE 16

Painted about 1478

PRIMAVERA

Uffizi Gallery, Florence

79⅞ x 123⅝"

This marvelous painting was ordered by Lorenzo di Pierfrancesco de' Medici for his villa at Castello, as was the later *Birth of Venus* (plate 18), which I believe was intended to hang opposite *Primavera* and to complete its meaning. The subject may have been suggested by Lorenzo's tutor, the Neoplatonist Marsilio Ficino (see back of book).

The modest lady in the center is Venus. At the right, one of the passing Hours, in a flowered dress, scatters blossoms. She is pushed into the grove by Flora, goddess of spring, from whose mouth flowers emerge, and who is in turn propelled by the puffing, winged wind god, Zephyrus. The blindfolded Cupid shoots a flaming arrow at the three transparently dressed Graces dancing in a ring. At the left, Mercury points upward with his staff to the golden fruit shining in the trees. Before the background of dark green foliage the pale, long-limbed figures move with a solemn and melodious grace, their golden tresses and diaphanous garments rippling about them, their eyes shining with awakened love, their feet barely pressing the carpet of flowers.

PLATE 17

Painted about 1486

A FLORENTINE LADY BEFORE VENUS AND THE GRACES

The Louvre, Paris

83½ x 111¾"

Despite attempts to identify her, we do not actually know who is the gentle bride in this fresco. She hopefully extends her wedding veil to Venus and the Three Graces who romp into the room from the left to confer their blessing. In the companion picture, also in The Louvre, Venus presents the bridegroom to the Seven Liberal Arts. These two frescoes decorated the open portico of a Florentine villa and were supposed to indicate the favors bestowed by the goddess of Love and Humanity upon her votaries.

Perhaps the simplicity of organization of these frescoes is explained by their architectural destination. But not even their purpose as wall paintings retards their incessant flow of line, and not even the heavy damage which the frescoes have suffered can destroy the sensitivity and delicacy of Botticelli's forms.

Painted about 1485

THE BIRTH OF VENUS

Uffizi Gallery, Florence

67⅜ x 109⅝"

The Birth of Venus was painted for Lorenzo di Pierfrancesco's villa, probably as a companion piece to the *Primavera* (plate 16), and in the sixteenth century they were seen together. Gombrich believes that its meaning, like that of the *Primavera,* is traceable to Ficino (see back of book). To give birth to Venus the sea was fertilized by Saturn; to Ficino this meant the fertilization of mankind by divinity and the birth of beauty in the human soul.

Although the pose was certainly inspired by classical statues of Venus, pagan voluptuousness is absent from this chaste and wistful creature, who patiently awaits the cloak that one of the Hours is about to cast around her. The Botticellian proportions show here their greatest exaggeration. Yet the entrancing flow of the long neck and sloping shoulders, the honeyed torrent of cascading hair about the exquisite body, transport the observer beyond the realm of anatomical accuracy.

*Plates 19 & 20
details of*
THE BIRTH OF VEN

PLATE 21

Painted 1488-90

THE ANNUNCIATION

Uffizi Gallery, Florence

59⅛ x 61⅜"

Like *The Madonna with Six Saints* (plate 23), this panel shows the gathering intensity of religious fervor that made Botticelli a willing listener to Savonarola. The sacred event, the very moment of the conception of Christ's human body, takes place in a room furnished only by the lectern at which Mary has been reading. Through the open door one looks into a closed garden, symbol of Mary's virginity. Beyond, a tree rises as if to fulfill the prophecy of Isaiah, "A shoot shall grow from Jesse's rod," and to foretell the Tree of the Cross (detail, plate 38). Mary sways like a sapling in the wind, her face pallid, her movements trancelike. The flow of Botticelli's line has now become a cascading rush, for it is the vehicle not only of a Renaissance love of beauty, but of a medieval Christianity revived in a new and burningly personal sense.

PLATE 22

Painted about 1482

THE ADORATION OF THE MAGI

National Gallery of Art, Washington, D.C.
(Mellon Collection)
27¾ x 40⅝"

More formal and more classical than the Uffizi version
(plate 12), this picture was probably painted during
Botticelli's stay in Rome. The free arrangements of the
earlier picture have given way to a great circle seen in
depth, broken only at the center of the side nearest
the spectator to give a clear view of the Virgin and
Child. The controlled curves of the kneeling figures are
reflected in the undulating hills and valleys of the
landscape background. Few of the faces seem to be
portraits.

The haunted arches and shattered wall of the Uffizi
picture have become an imposing Roman ruin. Even
the shed seems to have been planned to suggest at once
the pediment of a Roman temple and the beamed roof
of a Roman basilica. Before this structure the three
Kings and their train adore the Child in ritual
solemnity.

PLATES 23, 24, & 25

Painted about 1487

THE MADONNA WITH SIX SAINTS

Uffizi Gallery, Florence
98½ x 105½"

Painted for the Church of San Barnaba, this altarpiece
is the most monumental of Botticelli's few large-scale
panels. Youthful angels part a royal curtain of crim-
son and ermine before the Queen of Heaven, while
others hold her Son's nails and crown of thorns. On
the left, Saint Barnabas, patron saint of the commis-
sioning church, raises his hand in blessing and turns
toward the writing bishop, Saint Augustine, while
Saint Catherine of Alexandria, herself a princess, looks
upward to Mary. On the other side stand the patron
saint of Florence, John the Baptist, Saint Ignatius the
Bishop, and the archangel Michael, almost feminine in
his dreamy grace. (See the following two plates.)

Basically symmetrical, the composition is nonetheless delicately varied to avoid exact symmetry. The
density and richness of the colors and the luxurious
quality of the materials heighten the feeling of a court
ritual. Yet a closer approach reveals all the poignancy
one expects in Botticelli's faces. In the midst of royal
splendor the gaunt Baptist strikes a chill to the heart,
looking outward through unfocused eyes glazed with
pain (plate 34).

PLATE 26

Painted about 1490

THE MADONNA WITH THE BOOK

Poldi-Pezzoli Museum, Milan
22¾ x 15⅜"

Botticelli was responsible for the popularity of a new type of Madonna image, in which the Virgin and Child are occupied with an open book. The *Madonna of the Magnificat* (plate 2) is one of these literary pictures, many of which were executed by Botticelli's pupils. Here Mother and Child seem enchanted by the poetic phrases they have been reading, filled with the import of the prophetic passages, even enjoying the lettering in the great manuscript open before them. The Virgin, shown as writing in the *Madonna of the Magnificat,* here listens quietly while the Child expounds the sacred work. The crown of thorns encircles His left wrist, and His hand holds the nails which will pierce Him on the cross. But these symbols are treated with a new lightness. The Virgin is elegantly dressed, the crown of thorns is as dainty as the gold and crystal halos, and the delicate faces are modeled by a softer light than that of the solemn *Madonna of the Eucharist* (plate 11). It is as though the most sacred mysteries of the Passion could be discussed amid all the learning and refinement of a cultivated Florentine home.

PLATE 27

Painted about 1485

MARS AND VENUS

National Gallery, London

27½ x 68"

In this allegorical work painted for Botticelli's friends and neighbors, the Vespucci, Venus takes on the role of a powerful enchantress. Mars, the god of war, lies powerless in sleep, overcome by her spell. Baby satyrs play with his forgotten armor, helmet, and spear; demonstrate Mars's weakness by hanging a reed flute on one of his dangling fingers; blow softly into his ear through a conch shell. Wasps (Vespucci means "little wasps") buzz aimlessly over his head. The following passage from Marsilio Ficino (see back of book) may help to explain the picture: "Mars is outstanding in strength among the planets because he makes men stronger, but Venus masters him . . . Mars never masters Venus."

Botticelli's languor has reached a stage of bewitched enervation. The long format of the picture, the lithe limbs of the sleeping god, the light suffusing his features from below, the attenuated and delicate parallels of the folds of Venus' gown—all combine to produce a feeling of perfumed and unconquerable drowsiness.

PLATE 28

Painted about 1500

THREE MIRACLES OF SAINT ZENOBIUS

The Metropolitan Museum of Art, New York

26¼ x 59¼"

Many paintings from Botticelli's last phase show a new austerity, even harshness. The Saint Zenobius series, to which this panel belongs, create an inhuman setting of pale and barren architectural forms, within which the figures seem to hurtle back and forth with hysterical intensity. The composition is full of tensions. It is drawn out laterally to an uncomfortable degree, while the perspective in the center plunges sharply inward. Although the two sides of the architecture are strongly asymmetrical, the three little scenes balance almost exactly.

The architectural forms themselves with their staring, black windows are as abstract as if they had just come off an architect's drawing board. The painting abounds in startling, if accidental, resemblances to twentieth-century art; its fanatical precision suggests certain mechanistic painters of today, while the bleak piazza foreshadows the enigmatic settings of De Chirico.

PLATE 29

Painted about 1490-95

THE ANNUNCIATION

Collection Robert Lehman, New York

7½ x 12¼"

The Uffizi *Annunciation* (plate 21) was painted for a church altar. The present picture, like so many small versions of the subject by Botticelli, was done for a private patron and has the intimacy appropriate to a domestic interior. Extreme refinement of detail, precise integration of all the parts, and exquisite calculation of spatial relationships are typical of Botticelli's smaller works. The setting is a Renaissance villa, whose pilaster-lined corridors, coffered ceilings, and pedimented doorways, seen asymmetrically, form a complex spatial background for the figures. The Virgin has fallen to her knees, her head bent submissively, while the angelic messenger, entering with the light through the doorway, kneels before her. Miraculous gold rays from Heaven have pierced the very wall above the door and shine across the room, forming an intricate pattern of interlocking triangles with the angel's wings and the sharply receding lines of floor and ceiling.

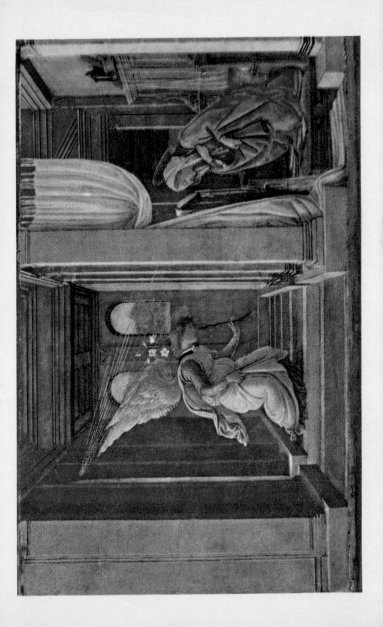

PLATE 30

Painted about 1495

THE LAST COMMUNION OF SAINT JEROME

The Metropolitan Museum of Art, New York

13 x 9"

The old chroniclers tell us that when Saint Jerome felt his death coming on he got up from his bed and knelt down on the ground to receive Communion, so weak that he had to be held up by other monks, yet insisting on delivering a long and passionate invocation of the Son of God, present in the Eucharist.

The Saint's dwelling place is a humble cottage woven of wattles. Over his bed covered with a sheepskin stands the crucifix before three palms, symbolic of Christ's sacrifice and of eternal life. Botticelli has drawn with the greatest delicacy the aged Saint whose whole being is concentrated on the heavenly promise contained in the white wafer, extended to him by the bending priest. The relief-like organization of the figures and the simplicity of the space make this little picture look more like a medieval than a Renaissance work.

PLATE 31

Painted in 1500

THE MYSTICAL NATIVITY

National Gallery, London

$42\frac{1}{8} \times 29\frac{1}{8}''$

Nowhere is the medievalism of Botticelli's later work more apparent than in this visionary painting. Its meaning is suggested by the Greek inscription at the top: it refers to the chaining of the devil a millennium and a half after the Nativity, as prophesied in the Revelation of Saint John the Divine. Botticelli offers the picture as hope for a tired generation. He has painted the Apocalyptic Woman who fled into the wilderness where God has prepared her a place (Revelation, xii). Under the rocks flee demons who dare not follow. Around the kneeling mother angels with olive branches summon shepherds to witness the Child, while others embrace three transfigured mortals. In the heavens twelve angels dance in a ring.

In its unreal linearity, its complete renunciation of Renaissance scale and proportion, its Gothic mysticism, this picture is indeed a return to medieval style. The embrace of peace, the circling patterns, are a ritual of surrender, assuaging the longings of the artist's lifetime.

Plate 32. ONE OF THE HOURS (*detail of color plate 16*)

Plate 33. VENUS *(detail of color plate 18)*

Plate 34. SAINT JOHN THE BAPTIST (*detail of color plate 23*)

Plate 35. SAINT AUGUSTINE (*detail of color plate 23*)

Plate 36. AN ANGEL. *Drawing. Uffizi Gallery, Florence*

Plate 37. ABUNDANCE. *Drawing. British Museum, London*

Plate 38. LANDSCAPE *(detail of color plate 21)*

Plate 39. PORTRAIT OF A WOMAN. *About 1494*
Pitti Palace, Florence

Plate 40. THE CALUMNY OF APELLES. *About 1494. Uffizi Gallery, Flo...*

Plate 41. PIETA. *After 1500. Alte Pinakothek, Munich*

Plate 42. MORDECAI AT THE GATE OF AHASUERAS' PALACE
About 1490. Collection Pallavicini, Rome

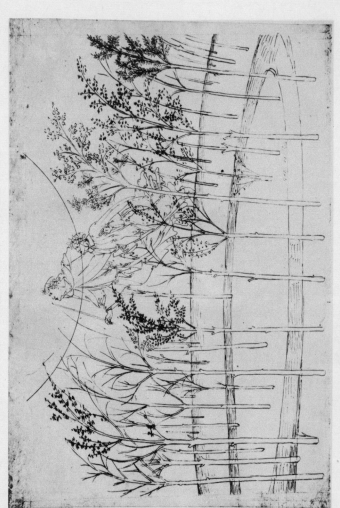

Plate 43. DANTE GUIDED BY BEATRICE FLOATS UP TO PARADISE

Drawing for Dante's DIVINE COMEDY. *Kupferstich-Kabinett, Berlin*

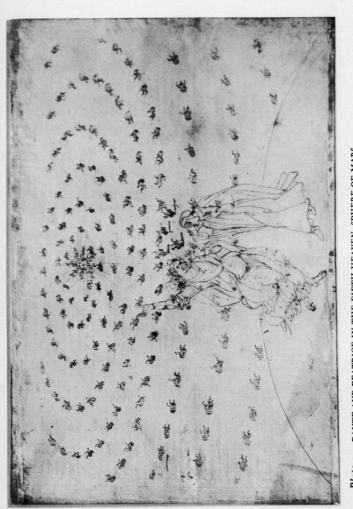

Plate 44. DANTE AND BEATRICE IN THE FIFTH HEAVEN, SPHERE OF MARS
Drawing for Dante's DIVINE COMEDY. *Kupferstich-Kabinett, Berlin*

BIOGRAPHICAL NOTES

1444/5	Sandro Botticelli (pronounced *bot-ti-CHEL-lee*) born in Florence.
1458/9	Probably studies with Fra Filippo Lippi.
1470	Earliest dated work, *Fortitude,* painted under the influence of Pollaiuolo.
about 1477/8	Develops his personal, linear style; begins famous series of mythological pictures.
1478	Commissioned to paint portraits of the rebels hanged after the Pazzi conspiracy.
1481	Commissioned by Pope Sixtus IV to paint frescoes for the Sistine Chapel in Rome.
1482	Probable date of return to Florence; further mythological and religious pictures.
about 1490	Begins to show new religious fervor, paints with greater emotional, dramatic intensity.
1491	Falls under spell of Savonarola.
1494	Expulsion of the Medici from Florence; Savonarola takes leading role in government; Botticelli's later style now formed.
1498	Execution of Savonarola; Botticelli now paints few pictures.
1510	Dies in Florence after a period of obscurity; buried in the Church of Ognissanti.

A NOTE ON MARSILIO FICINO
AND THE SYMBOLISM OF VENUS

Today we tend to think of Venus mainly as "the Goddess of Love." To Botticelli's audience, however, she had a multitude of meanings: in addition to her classical divinity, her symbolism was colored by such traditions as medieval moral allegory, astrology, courtly love, and Neoplatonic philosophy. For an understanding of the *Primavera* (plate 16) and *The Birth of Venus* (plate 18), E. H. Gombrich has suggested that we turn to the Neoplatonist Marsilio Ficino (1433-1499), the tutor of Lorenzo di Pierfrancesco de' Medici, for whose villa the paintings were executed. The following passages are from Ficino's letters to the young Lorenzo:

"Venus, that is to say Humanity . . . is a nymph of excellent comeliness, born of heaven and more than others beloved by God all highest. Her soul and mind are Love and Charity, her eyes Dignity and Magnanimity, the hands Liberality and Magnificence, the feet Comeliness and Modesty. The whole, then, is Temperance and Honesty, Charm and Splendor. Oh, what exquisite beauty! How beautiful to behold! My dear Lorenzo, a nymph of such nobility has been wholly given into your hands. If you were to unite with her in wedlock and claim her as yours, she would make all your years sweet.

"Venus . . . is the Mother of Grace, of Beauty, and of Faith. . . . Beauty is nothing but Grace, a Grace, I say, composed of three Graces . . . which descend in a similar way from three celestial powers."

Another passage from Ficino may explain the *Mars and Venus* (see commentary for plate 27).

SOME OTHER BOOKS
ABOUT BOTTICELLI

Bernard Berenson. *The Italian Painters of the Renaissance.* New York, Phaidon, 1953

E. H. Gombrich. "Botticelli's Mythologies," *Journal of the Warburg and Courtauld Institutes* (London), 1945, pp. 6-60
(A new interpretation of Botticelli's mythological works)

H. P. Horne. *Sandro Botticelli.* London, G. Bell and Sons, 1908
(The basic work on Botticelli's style and chronology)

Lionello Venturi. *Botticelli.* New York, Phaidon, 1937

Yukio Yashiro. *Sandro Botticelli.* London, The Medici Society, 1925

ACKNOWLEDGMENTS

In a book of art, it seems particularly fitting to acknowledge the work of craftsmen who contribute to its making. The color plates were made by Litho-Art, Inc., New York. The lithography is from the presses of The Meehan-Tooker Co., Inc., New York and the binding has been done by F. M. Charlton Co., New York. The paper was made by P. H. Glatfelter Co., Spring Grove, Pa. Our deepest indebtedness is to the museums, galleries, and private collectors who graciously permitted the reproduction of their paintings, drawings, and sculpture.